Spending the Winter

Other Books of Interest from St. Augustine's Press

Joseph Bottum, *The Decline of the Novel*

Joseph Bottum, *The Second Spring*

Joseph Bottum, *The Fall and Other Poems*

Numa Fustel de Coulanges, (Faith Bottum, translator)
The Ancient City

Jeremy Black, *The Importance of Being Poirot*

Jeremy Black, *In Fielding's Wake*

Marvin R. O'Connell, *Telling Stories that Matter: Memoirs and Essays*

Rollin A. Lasseter, *The Cast of Valor*

Ralph McInerny, *Shakespearean Variation*

Ralph McInerny, *The Soul of Wit: Some Poems*

Anne Drury Hall, *Where the Muses Still Haunt: The Second Reading*

David Lowenthal, *Slave State: Rereading Orwell's 1984*

Gene Fendt, *Camus' Plague: Myth for Our World*

John Poch, *God's Poems:*
The Beauty of Poetry and the Christian Imagination

Roger Scruton, *The Politics of Culture and Other Essays*

Roger Scruton, *The Meaning of Conservatism: Revised 3rd Edition*

Roger Scruton, *An Intelligent Person's Guide to Modern Culture*

Allen Mendenhall, *Shouting Softly: Lines on Law, Literature, and Culture*

Gabriel Marcel, *The Invisible Threshold: Two Plays by Gabriel Marcel*

Will Morrisey, *Shakespeare's Politic Comedy*

Will Morrissey, *Herman Melville's Ship of State*

Winston Churchill, *The River War*

Spending the Winter

Joseph Bottum

St. Augustine's Press

South Bend, Indiana

Manufactured in the United States of America.

1 2 3 4 5 6   27 26 25 24 23 22

Library of Congress Control Number: 2022939585

Paperback ISBN: 978-1-58731-815-3
Ebook ISBN: 978-1-58731-816-0

∞ The paper used in this publication meets the minimum requirements of the American National Standard for Information Sciences – Permanence of Paper for Printed Materials, ANSI Z39.48-1984.

St. Augustine's Press
www.staugustine.net

For Heather Hyde

Table of Contents

IV: Occasionals

V: Spending the Winter

I: The Morning Watch

Easter Morning
for René Girard

Quick as dawn, the dogwoods have raised
Improbable awnings, christened with rain.
Thrusts of witch-hazel, stands of rue,
And there—*there*, across the stream,
In the shade of those dark-lichened rocks—
White phlox and geranium strain
To reach the angled light. One bright
Morning, a clean April day,
Amazes familiar paths with a green
Tangle and baizes the winter's stain.

Faster each Easter, my daughter flies
Past tumbled mounds where brambles grow.
The bloodroot flowers near her feet
As delicate as bible leaves,
And slow, persistent ivy kindles
On old trees. The year will know
A fresh redemption—*Burning green,*
The greenwoods glow—till ash
And thorn fall back to sleep,
Counterpaned again with snow.

Beneath these trees, with ragged knives,
Cold priests once tried to wake the leaf,
The root, the branch: the frozen world
That needs new life for spring.
A lamb, a child—the shrouds of snow

Would melt in their warm blood, as grief
By grief, pain by vengeful pain,
We paid the sacrificial debt
That swells with each repaying death.
And where in time is time's relief?

My daughter runs by the brief flowers:
Touch-me-nots among the stones,
Bluebells and sorrels, Solomon's seal.
Every spring pretends a pity
For all the pretty, short-lived things.
Last night I watched the fire zones,
The bombers' plumes and tracer rounds,
Blooms of war on the TV news.
And now in these green trees I see
The graves of gods and a grove of bones.

History labors, a worn machine
Sick with torsion, ill-meshed,
And every repair of an old fault
Ruptures something new. The sacred
Knife no longer hallows woods,
But winter's blood still springs refreshed
And an altered world still summons death.
As long as we endure ourselves,
Innocence will come to grief
And mercy must remain unfleshed.

The parish bells begin their carols,
Down through the trees like flourished prayer
The Easter call resounding. Time
Reaches forward, hungry for winter,
And what will save my daughter when even

4

Hope is caught in the ancient snare?
A cold fear waits—till all that had fallen,
All that was lost, rudely broken,
Crossed in love, comes rising, *rising*,
On the breath of the new spring air.

What Falls Was Green

What falls was green. Now not.
Winter wastes what summer
Wrought—brought from root,
As root from seed, and seed
From flower, stem, and sprout.
All brightness leans to dark
And doubt: each leaf a candle
Guttered out, a guess
At something spring had sought
Then lost among the weeds.
We mean our thoughts and words,
Our deeds, to last: to best
The summer drifting past
And reach beyond the year.
But what remains is mostly
Loss—the sapless ghost
Of work that we have left
Undone, the promise we
Forgot. What falls was green.
Now not.
     Now not.

Still Life

Then the roses were in bloom.
Are still.
    Are still—
We trust so much the future will . . .
Will likely come at all, I guess
We mean. A graceful acquiescence
Brings this green to red, this stem
To bloom: the lenient gift, the clemency
That we assume in time.

So if the trellised roses climb
Riotous and tangled there
Along the garden walls, all careless
Of the coming fall—or if
The hybrid here, our hieroglyph
Of calm consent, still waits unworried
Within this table vase, unhurried
By the *now* that breaks from past
To past, to past, then much will last,
Perhaps, and love survive the day.

But if I risk a glance away,
Will I return to find you still—
    Turn in time to find you still—
Waiting here in the sunlit room
Among the roses, still in bloom?

Bliss and Blunder

Worthless things and things of wonder
    Are fish in a single lake—
For much of bliss is caught by blunder,
    And joy by some mistake.

The Hidden Life
for Dana Gioia

Sometimes on evening walks you hear
    The whispers from old wells,
Those almost-words that rivers speak—
    A quiet voice that tells
Of small, secluded things. Like murmured
    Prayers from churchmen's stalls
Or what the marbled echoes say,
    It rises and it falls.
And you may follow when it calls,

Or you may think to wait. The green
    At dusk seems deeper than
The green at dawn. Beyond the gate
    A garden opens on
Long shadows overgrown with leaves
    And lilac nunneries
Between the gravel paths, where sparrows
    Seek their tenebraes.
And you may follow, if you please,

Or keep to public streets. Against
    The bruit of busy day,
The private houses close their eyes.
    A few small panes betray
High bookshelves in a well-lit room,
    A woman sweeping floors,

A glimpse of some attentive boy
　　At work at evening chores.
And you may follow through those doors,

Or you may turn aside. In lines
　　Of black between the flames,
A fire writes against its light.
　　Dry hopes, forgotten fames,
The traceless works of childless men—
　　All printed there to read.
The cinders spell the deeper night,
　　Dark need inside dark need.
And you may follow where they lead,

Or you may look away.

Ascetic's Prayer

Lord, find us better things to do
Than talk of bodies, two by two,
And all the frenzies that ensue.

Make us angels, beasts, or stones:
Something deaf to creaks and groans,
The slosh and sway around our bones.

Lord, save us from biography:
The stench of time, the fetid tree
Of life, relived in memory.

Self-acclaimed and self-excused,
Self-absorbed and self-abused—
Beloved lovers, self-seduced:

We labor for our vile supply
Of self-deceit. That slick word *I*
Is always preface for some lie.

I hate, I love—O Lord Above:
Ensouled in bodies, hand in glove,
With all the wrinkled fit thereof,

We are unclean in word and deed,
In how we shit and how we feed,
In what we boast and what we plead.

Lord, best of all is not to be.
I'll swim out past the reef of me
To feel the current pulling free

And drown myself in the selfless sea.

Tardy

We never exactly mean to dawdle
Or let the day slip by.
I stopped at the pond for just a moment
To see if the mallards would try

The sunflower seeds I'd found in a cupboard.
I didn't stay too long.
But time moves strangely near to water,
The careless current strong,

And there are fish to watch in the shallows,
With small new signs of spring:
The green-touched reeds and willow catkins
Like down on a duckling's wing.

And now I'm hurried, pressed and tardy,
With penalties to pay,
Returned to the world of busy people
And clocks that keep the day.

The Morning Watch

I was sure that I would stay
Awake last night, lasting through
To daybreak and the Easter light—
A dawning through the dimmed stained glass
Of Lazarus Rising, Jerusalem's Daughters,
St. James in shades of red and blue.
Feigning wakefulness, I traced
The curve of lines in the high ceiling.
And there, near rows of doused candles,
I fell asleep on the hardwood pew.

Last night I proudly told my parents
That I could stay awake to keep
The Easter vigil, not just my hour.
And when I awoke, the night had passed.
Through eastern windows, the morning twilight,
Stained red and blue, had begun to seep.
A corduroy jacket covered me.
I flailed awake, and my grandfather, watching
His hour, wrapped me in his arms.
My parents had gone home to sleep.

When I was eight, I fell asleep
And missed my watch on Easter night.
My father, grandfather, Mrs. Byrne,
Who covered me with her warm coat
In St. James' Church—Where are they now?
Time has doused the kind and bright

Who watched for me. In passing years,
They have all gone home to sleep.
Only elsewhere will they rise
To new air and the dayspring light.

II: Imitations

Floret Silva Nobilis

The noble forest flourishes
As sylvan folioles uncoil,
While tender vines and vernal flowers
Burgeon from the fertile soil.

Christ, these spring woods grow so hollow.
Nothing got but winter's lack.
Loveless, lovelorn unbelovèd:
Never will my friend come back.

Never. No one. Nothing more.
Feathers wafted out to sea.
Why, my love, *despicis domum,*
Now not coming home for me?

---

l.11 despicis domum—Latin for *[you] despise the house*

Doves

after Raimundo Correia's 1883 Brazilian sonnet, "As Pombas"

At dawn, the first awakened dove will fly.
And then another. Another. A pair. Then dozens:
The battering wings of brothers, sisters, cousins—
All rising fresh to claim the sun-brushed sky.

But in the afternoon, the stiff winds pry
Back from distant trees the doves in their dozens.
Unsettled droves of brothers, sisters, cousins
Must turn again for home, not knowing why.

Out from the restless hearts where love had been,
Their secret hopes take wing and flee again
Just as doves from lofts at dawn had vanished.

Amidst the blue of morning's adolescence
They flew—then fluttered back to home's quiescence.
And from their dove-gray breasts their dreams are banished.

O Portuguese

for Lorena and Faith, Brazilian wife and daughter

She cursed like an angel beneath the favèla trees.
The sibilant scorn of nectar and poison flowed
From blood-red lips. A playful Atlantic breeze
Brushed back dark hair. The brilliant morning slowed.

On a hill in Rio de Janeiro I heard
A beautiful stranger berate her unfaithful lover.
The ghosts of long-dead sailors and poets stirred
To speak again old words for her voice to recover.

O Portuguese, the final flower of Latin,
You are a butcher's knife on a bed of satin:
Poor but rich with sorrow, sweet and wild,

The sound of Magellan when he braved far oceans,
The language of Camões and love's devotions,
The tongue my daughter first heard say, *My child.*

Choriambs and Trisyllabics:
Four Englishings of Neo-Latin Hexameter

I. Seven Years Away from Paris
after George Buchanan's 1567 "Desiderium Lutetiae"

These seven new frosts, seven fresh snows,
    O love, all these seven long years
Are gone from me now, time unredeemed,
    Each dragging a summer along.
Slow seasons of sleet, seasons of swelter,
    Sevens arrayed in platoons—
But nothing is changed, nothing reformed,
    To lessen the ache that I feel.

Unstilled is the tune, heard at first dawn,
    As throngs of bright songbirds returned
To skirr the young grass, fresh for the spring,
    And court in the dazzles of dew.
My love is my noon, morning and dusk.
    And when the sun's shadows distend,
Engulfing the day, dark's little death,
    All men are afraid—except me.
For still you are there, draped in my dreams,
    To share the chimeras of sleep.
In dreams we can dance, laugh and embrace.
    In dreams we restore the old days.

But sleepers soon wake, cares are renewed.
    I stumble each morning through town.

Like boxes of pain, tombs for undead,
　　The houses are haunts of the lost.
I trudge through the fields, dogged, alone,
　　In useless escape from myself,
As up the rough hills, through the dim woods,
　　I shoulder my drearisome weight.

And sometimes on cliffs, watching the sea
　　That thrashes itself into foam,
I shout at deaf storms, scream at blind skies,
　　My yearning and soul-severed need:
Please carry me out, over the waves,
　　To glide on the saltwater glass.
O nymphs of the sea, smoothly I'd sail
　　To home in the harbor I love.
But safety be damned: Storm-wracked will do
　　If dangers were speeding me on.

The wind hears me mourn: *Fortunate breeze,*
　　To fly with a breath to the north.
I pray that the clouds clear a swift path,
　　No Pyrenees bruising your wings,
As hurrying home, rushing to France,
　　You carry the word of my faith.

How often I've asked seabirds in flight
　　For news of my distant desire.
Far Paris, my love, city of light—
　　The sweet *Marianne* of my song—
Does she still recall days that we shared?
　　The nights of carousal and cheer?
But scraping the waves breaking at sea,
　　The great gulls all spiral away.

My rural retreat, Portuguese idyll,
  Offers Acadian scenes:
The piping of boys, dancing of girls,
  The holiday songs of a feast—
All tainted and spoiled, weakened and marred,
  By thought of my fair Marianne. . . .

A pair of new towns, Portugal's own
  Coìmbra and Évora tried
To lure me away, draw me from you,
  With love-hungry whispers and cries.
Like winter to spring, wizened to young,
  They cannot compete with your charms.

Coìmbra reflects, down at the river,
  Watching herself in its mirror.
Lovely, she thinks, preening in place,
  Before she will turn to exclaim,
Why waste all your love, yearning for what
  Your agony never obtains?
Why spurn the fresh buds, cherries and grapes:
  The blessings I furnish for you?

Swift Évora twirls, dancing at feasts,
  Pretending that I cannot see.
And tapping her foot, swaying her hips,
  She sings of the judgments of fate:
When hunters chase hares, scorning near game,
  They turn empty-handed for home.
So fishermen find nothing to catch
  If only the fanciest fish
Will satisfy tastes grown too refined.
  Come dance with the one who is near. . . .

All this and much more, Évora sings,
    All this fair Coìmbra confides,
To ears that are deaf, eyes that are blind,
    To fall to their Portuguese wiles.
For dogs will kiss wolves, doves will greet hawks,
    And deer will adore lions' claws,
Ere Évora's songs, come-hither dances,
    Alter my cynosure heart.
Coìmbra's allure, shameless appeal,
    Won't change my Parisian desire.
Do fish leave the sea, winds flee the sky?
    Does Marianne fade from my thoughts?
For she holds the spark, mistress of fire,
    That she, only she, can inflame.

2. A London Frost Fair
after William Baker's 1634 "Descriptio Brumae"

The winter's brief day, wearied and weak,
    Has finished the year's final run:
Halfhearted light, flyover flare,
    And feeble old Phoebus is done.

The lifeless low fields, listless and wan,
    Asleep in a sheeting of frost,
Woebegone shrubs, bareheaded trees,
    Their summers of greenery lost:

Yes, Earth has endured insults before,
    Withstanding the blizzards and cold—
Rimmed with the rime ice of the time,
    Resembling the grizzled and old.

But worse than before, winter this year
    Has stormed the slow rivers with snow.
Hardened to ice, water like glass
    Is swift to a motionless flow.

And since the new year gives them a foothold,
    Freezing a pathway of ice,
Wandering folk walk on the Thames,
    Astounded by winter's device.

With chattering calls, roughhousing brawls,
    The boys and the girls at their play,

London is charmed—novelty's gift
    Of mischief and mirth for the day.

So, smoking their pipes, barkeeps will build
    Their river-ice taverns and rooms.
Drinkers soon spill, nosediving down
    To sweep at bright snow like new brooms.

The boatman is set back on his heels,
    Unable to ply at his oar.
Hunting instead, shooting at birds,
    He wages a countryside war.

The faraway hills, fleeced all in white,
    The snow-gabled houses in town—
Steam from our breath, frosting in air,
    And icicles drip-dropping down:

The cold has become festival fare,
    As laughing the crowds scrape away
Icy new beards, hair-braids of snow,
    While holding the hoarfrost at bay.

So Londoners play blustery games,
    And leaving a hearth-heated home,
Take to the streets, thronging the squares—
    Astray from their day jobs to roam

In search of fresh sport, jostling to join
    Tomfoolery's revels and show.
Football breaks out—scrums on the ice,
    The contest of feet in the snow.

But others decide battle is best,
    And packing the snow into balls,
Face off against friends on the river,
    Trumpeting impudent calls.

Still others will choose wintery arts
    And raise up cold figures to fright
Boys in the lanes, girls in the mews,
    And old folk who footslog at night.

So there a cruel bear opens its maw,
    While here fearsome lions will roar,
Statues of snow, artfully shaped,
    Of sea-monsters crawling to shore.

The season had seemed steadfastly turning
    Day to a desolate place.
London instead, laughing at play,
    Has tempered the cold into grace.

Thus bad comes to good, years are redeemed,
    For nothing is lost from God's hold.
Winter will fall, reaching its end,
    And spring in due time will unfold.

3. The Transit of Venus

after "Quid fugis ah formosa tuas?"—a poem the young astronomer Jeremiah Horrocks set in his 1639 prose work, Venus in sole visa, *the first accurate observation and mathematical calculation of the path of the planet.*

Why do you flee, Beautiful One,
    Abandoning lovers and friends?
Why must you leave, why go astray,
    Concealing the gift of your face?
Why do you grace regions ungrateful?
    Europe still yearns for your touch.
Why such a haste, wantonly wasting
    Wonders on strangers at dusk?
They do not care, they will not tend
    To care for a tender young girl.
Stay with us here, here we will hurry
    Flowers to furnish your bed—
Resting secure, you may recover
    Strength that was lost in your trek.

Goodness deprived, Goddess denied,
    We wretched remain in the east:
Merciless Skies, Heavens Unbending,
    Scarcely allowed a last kiss.
Cold nights will fall, dark dreams arise.
    America clutches her now.
Gnarled in its trees, caught in its woods,
    The light of bright Venus will dwell.
Heavenly One, Beautiful Goddess,

Under your rule far away
May the untamed, wandering ones,
    Americans lured to the west,
Learn to be calm, learn to be gentle,
    Roughness transfigured to peace.

Writing with zeal, eager in thought,
    As far as permitted I've traced
Arcs of your dark onerous trails
    Traversing celestial realms.
Goddess, this book—figuring patterns
    Sketched in the heavens above—
Sets as a vow, marks as a pledge,
    Astronomy's circular paths.
Children unborn, kindred to come:
    A hundred and twenty new springs,
Summers and falls, winters in turn,
    Refreshes the fairest of stars.
Then may you see Venus in transit,
    Crossing the face of the Sun.

4. Epitaph for a Dog
loosely after Vincent Bourne's 1724 "Epitaphium in Canem"

Now resting at last, here will I stay,
    The leaves turning yellow and red,
While waiting for him, joined once again,
    To sleep with his hand on my head.

The surest of guards, sharpest of guides,
    I kept to my master's slow pace.
Down labyrinth lanes, dangerous ways,
    I watched for a threatening face—

Or folk to entreat, hands that might give
    A crust for my master to eat,
As tied with some twine, tugging a string,
    I threaded our way to his seat.

Then "Wolfie," he'd say—terrible name:
    A dog is more faithful and fit—
But "Wolfie," he'd say, "stay by my side,"
    And down at his feet I would sit

As calling aloud, moaning of fate,
    He cried to the crowd by the park
Of blindness and night, eyes that can't see,
    Beseeching their coins in his dark,

Some pitiful pence, all that we need,
    And often enough they would come.

My master, a poor, hunger-hunched man,
  Would give to me half of each crumb.

And so we survived, filling the hours
  With morsels and feasts of small bites.
As passers-by thinned, homeward I'd lead,
  His days unseen fading to nights.

But aging at last, slowing and weak,
  I lost my sure grip on his leash.
And now I must wait, hoping that soon
  He'll meet me to rest here in peace.

But lest he forget, losing his way,
  My master has raised this small mound
Where digging by hand, shaping by touch,
  He set me so gently to ground.

Saro's Love Song

in homage to Sardasht Osman, assassinated in 2010 at age 23

I am in love with Masoud's daughter—
Masoud Barzani: the man you see
Here and there, the man who says
He is my president. I want
Him for my father-in-law. I want
His son for my brother-in-law. I want
His lovely daughter to marry me.

If I were married to Masoud's daughter,
We'd spoon and honeymoon in Paris.
We'd visit her uncle's American mansion.
We'd leave my backstreet room in Arbil
For upmarket places in Sari Rash.
We'd take my poor, unfancied sister
To fancy stores in a fancy car.

If I were married to Masoud's daughter,
My mother would have Italian doctors
Nodding wisely while she complained
About her swollen feet and heart.
My uncles would have swank offices.
My nieces and nephews would all grow fat
In rich positions for the state.

If I were married to Masoud's daughter,
I'd put my pensionless father in charge
Of all our Kurdish militia troops.

I'd name my little brother as head
Of special forces—the luckless boy
Who's finished school but has no job
And talks of leaving Kurdistan.

My friends say: Saro, let it go.
You've never even met the girl
You're babbling on and on about.
The Barzanis, old Mustafa's tribe,
Are people who kill whatever they want.
And you'll be what they want to kill,
Unless you shut up about their daughter.

But why should I be silent now?
My father warred against Saddam
With Masoud's brother—I swear on his knife:
Three nights on the mountain they stood together.
Masoud says he's my president,
But when has he ever left his palace
To visit old soldiers in Arbil's slums?

I wonder what my mother-in-law
Looks like. I checked around online,
And I could find, easily enough,
Photos of other leaders' wives—
But never Masoud's. Perhaps she's shy?
Without knowing, I can't decide
Who should help arrange my marriage.

At first I thought I would take an imam,
A good, respectable whitebeard fellow,
And a few of the old militiamen
To ask for the hand of Masoud's daughter.

But everyone says I should use instead
Some of Saddam's collaborators,
The murderers and ethnic cleansers

Masoud seems to like so much.
Perhaps my busy brother-in-law
Will mention me in a press release
So my father-in-law can learn who I am.
Or maybe that pop-star Dashni will sing
About my love for Masoud's daughter.
She's always mooning around these days.

I am in love with Masoud's daughter—
Masoud Barzani: the man you see
Here and there, the man who says
He is my president. I want
Him for my father-in-law. I want
His son for my brother-in-law. I want
His lovely daughter to marry me.

Some Souls

after Victor Hugo's 1840 "Comme dans les étangs"

Sometimes among the elms we see a pool
Both bright and dark. And so sometimes a soul:
The sunlit sky, so clean, reflected there
Upon the surface, tinted blue and clear;
And down below, the silt disturbed by storms,
Where dark things wake from sleep and crawl in swarms.

III: Trifles

Going Steady

Like a horse with a cart down the pitch of a hill
And the jolt each back-leaned step,
And the side-slip slide to the edge of the ditch
And the brakeless careen down the last of the slope,

Our lives now slow on the flat, smooth road.

An Adulterer's Introspection

Curious, as Sherlock once remarked:
The conscientious watchdog never barked.

The Logician's Lament

The premises we thought we knew:
All men are mortal. Love is, too.
But premises need not be true.

So first the syllogistic form:
All hair is red, all hair is warm—
These starting points, as much untrue

As she has been to me again,
Nonetheless by logic's spin
Issue in a thought that's true:

Something warm is also red.
I know she warms some other's bed.
If only thinking were less true

Or love had left the heart unwooed,
The cruel mind would not conclude
That absent lovers prove untrue.

Reading by Osmosis

Well . . .

Mark Twain, Hart Crane,
    And Ursula K. LeGuin—
    We've mastered their books with a difficult trick:
    We've read them outside in.

Percy B. Shelley and Machiavelli
    And Norman Vincent Peale—
    We've never tried opening one of their books.
    We know them by their feel.

Does reading seem boring? Does reading seem hard?
    Does reading seem too precocious?
    Just pick up a book and give it a twirl.
    You'll learn it by osmosis.

Because . . .

Osmosis is the mostest.
    Osmosis is the best.
    Osmosis is the closest thing to reading without rest.

Osmosis means absorbing.
    Osmosis means so much.
    Osmosis means we're soaking up the books we barely touch.

We bobble, bounce, and throw them.
  We never even look.
  Osmosis means we know them without opening a book.

You know . . .

My sister osmoted *The Mill on the Floss,*
  A wonderful book, and gave me a gloss.
My brother osmoted *The Lord of the Rings,*
  A story of insects with thousands of wings—
  Or was that a book called *Lord of the Flies?*
Oh, well, we're getting wise
  By learning the things that osmosis now brings.

We'll juggle the books *Little Women* and *Men*
  (They're all about dwarves in a mountainy den)
And throw in a copy of *Watership Down*
  (Concerning a boat and some sailors who drown),
And then . . . we'll run to the bookstore again.

We boast! We boast!
  Osmosis is the most
    Phenomenal way
      To read today
        While eating jam and toast!

We shout! We plead!
  Osmosis we will need
    For playing jacks
      And munching snacks
        And dancing while we read!
So . . .

Rebecca West and Edgar Guest:
  We'll never be certain which one is the best.
Christopher Smart and Jean-Paul Sartre:
  Just think of the wonders they have to impart.
John Donne and Thom Gunn:
  Osmoting them both is a gallon of fun.
Somerset Maugham and L. Frank Baum,
  Josiah Royce and James Joyce,
    John Bunyan and Damon Runyon,
      Graham Greene and Molly Keane,
      Tom Paine and Ed McBain,
    Ring Lardner and John Gardner,
  Alice Munro and Arthur Rimbaud,
And oh, hundreds of others we know.

Because . . .

Osmosis is the mostest.
  Osmosis is the best.
    Osmosis is the closest thing to reading without rest.

Osmosis means absorbing.
  Osmosis means so much.
    Osmosis means we're soaking up the books we barely touch.

We hold them to our noses.
  We brush them with our clothes.
    We're learning by osmosis when we tap them with our toes.

We pile them on the table.
  We slide them on the floor.
    We stack them into stairways, and we climb up for some more.

We bobble, bounce, and throw them.
  We never even look.
  Osmosis means we know them without opening a book.

My Last Dutch Oven

an updating of Robert Browning's "My Last Duchess" (1842)

That's my last Dutch oven in the sink,
Looking as though it still were good. I think
Its age a wonder, now. Le Creuset made
It—pricy but, they said, the highest grade.
The years have scratched its finish, dulled its shine.
Stains show up when I deglaze with wine,
And gone are days when it was good for meat:
A pot—how shall I say?—too quick to heat.
I used it for a while for stovetop fries.
Then cooking mostly stopped. I caramelize
In stock pots now. I know I'll have to buy
Some replacement for my shepherd's pie.
Still, Amazon will ship new pots for free,
Which Lodge, perhaps, will cast in iron for me.

IV: Occasionals

Four Seasons
a graduation poem

I. Winter
(in a grim tetrameter)

God hunts old men out of season,
Winters them before they fall.
Time begins to lose cohesion.
The caller walks behind the call.

A dance begins before its dancer.
Enchantments thrill before their spell.
On weathered palms, a chiromancer
Reads what eyes already tell.

In cataracts of tears, the aging,
Still focused on a fruitless cause,
Forget that once, young spirits raging,
They raced to claim the world's applause.

Beset and battered, they have ended
Bombarded by time's grenadiers.
The tallest towers, proud and splendid,
Still fall to storms of savage years.

Is all we have to learn from living,
Despite devices we contrive,

That cold December's unforgiving,
And we will not escape alive?

Four Seasons—Phi Beta Kappa poem, Princeton University, 2022.
l.4 caller—Wilbur, "Mayflies."
l.5 dancer—Yeats, "Among School Children."
l.9 cataracts of tears: Guarini, "The Faithful Shepherd."

2. Spring
(in a warmer ballad meter)

April wants to think it's cruel,
  Rainy, dank, and grim.
But no one is sufficient fool
  To give in to its whim.

Oh, death is mixed up with the soil,
  And where some Caesar bled
The hyacinth and bluebell toil
  To bring to life the dead.

But no one minds. It is the season
  Of green and limber days,
A time of laughter for no reason
  And yearning's eager blaze.

The lilacs banish necromancy
  With rose and lady's glove.
Come spring, a student's bookish fancy
  Lightly turns to love.

Each April tunes discordant heartstrings,
  Blushing robins' breasts,
As fresh-faced gangs of wanton lapwings
  Strut and puff their chests.

Young Goliards in their college classrooms
  (That's you, or what you've been)

All learn to name the culture's heirlooms,
   Reciting *where* and *when*.

Wise fools, they think there's time for judging
   God and sex and death.
The spring, they know, should be ungrudging—
   A joy with every breath.

l.1 April . . . cruel: Eliot, *The Wasteland* 1.
l.6 some Caesar: Fitzgerald, *Rubaiyat* 19.
ll.15–19 fancy . . . lapwings: Tennyson, "Locksley Hall."
l.21 Goliards: Medieval university poets.

3. Summer
(in sprightlier Alexandrines)

The summer opens slow, as graduation parts,
In gowns and mortarboards, the friends of liberal arts,
The engineering kids, computer-science geeks,
Religion's novice monks, the Greek-and-Latin freaks.

And yet, you're forced to hear, before you leave the quad,
The graduation speech—and then you must applaud
Sententious sentiment, the opposite of song,
And like a wounded snake, it drags its length along.
There's something in these days that wants to make us dabble
In pleonastic bleats and brain-dead psychobabble.
Beware such words as *sync*, but flee *holistic* first.
Thought leader, Meta, Think outside the box—but worst
Of all are *synergy, new normal, ideates*:
They mar the soul and bruise the heart of your classmates.

Ye sacred Bards, that to your harps' melodious strings
Once sang poetic truths to mend the minds of kings,
Bestow a season off, to summer with the Muse—
To choose the odd, to trust in God, to take short views,

Before the year is washed again with autumn's hues
And winter's news.

---

l.8 wounded snake . . . along: Pope, *Essay on Criticism* 2.
l.15 Ye sacred . . . strings: Drayton, *Poly-Olbion* 31.
l.18 Choose . . . views: Auden, "Under Which Lyre."

4. Autumn
(in the blank verse of a philosophical pentameter)

Back in 1970, Saul Kripke,
Then Princeton's great philosopher, observed
That Phosphorus, the dawning star of morning,
And Hesperus, the evening star at dusk,
Are both, in truth, the twilight planet Venus.
The sentence *Phosphorus is Hesperus*
Is thus a logical necessity,
Although that took millennia to learn.

And what if many necessary truths
Are similar—both logical and waiting?
Think, for instance, of the proposition
That freedom of the will requires death.
The logic's quick enough: Free will takes change,
And every change needs something's dissolution.

But other consequences may unfold
In time. The fact that all that lives must die
Unburdens us and eases small dismay.
Undoes ambition, greed, the rush of fame.
Unkindness, too: The price of living long
Is burying your parents, teachers, friends.
Be gentle. Everyone you know is dying.
Be light of touch. Everyone's an orphan,
Soon enough.
                         And take what time provides:
A chance to seek the beautiful and wise,

To look to God, to live with graceful rites.
These come with death, like crimson leaves, and some
Will catch your eye and strike you as they fall.

In ancient Roman triumphs, servants murmured
To generals and emperors, *Remember*
You are mortal, lest the cheering crowd
Fan belief that they had turned to gods.
Now poets are those servants, come to say,

> *This is your Morning Star—that you must die.*
> *This is your Evening Star—that you are free.*

And Love, like Venus in her transit, marks
The way.

---

l.7 logical necessity: Kripke, *Naming and Necessity* 3.
l.16 All . . . die: Shakespeare, *Hamlet* 1.2.
ll.26–27 some . . . fall: Robinson, "Luke Havergal."
ll.28 triumphs: Beard, *The Roman Triumph* 85–92.
ll.29–30 Remember . . . mortal: "Memento mori," in pithy Latin.
l.35 her transit: Horrocks, "Quid fugis ah formosa tuas?"

Some Come to See the Lord
a Christmas carol

Some come because as children
    They sang old Christmas songs.
Some come because as children
    They suffered hurts and wrongs.
The wounded, poor, and shattered—
The heartsick, lost, and battered:
Some come for life restored.
Some come to see the Lord.

Along the city sidewalks
    Cold Santas ring their bells.
Along the city sidewalks
    The storefront music swells.
So much leads to the manger:
The cheer you lent a stranger,
The gift for no reward,
The love you gave the Lord.

Across the fields in winter,
    The snow lies soft and clean.
Across the fields in winter,
    A new-made world is seen.
We will escape the sadness.
There lives now grace and gladness
And peace beyond the sword:
This child who is the Lord.

A storm of angels swirling
    While great kings kneel in straw,
A storm of angels swirling
    While shepherds watch in awe:
The world is charged with glory
And changed by faith's new story.
Some come for love outpoured.
Some come to see the Lord.

The Wind Unschooled:
Two Verses for My Godchildren

I. Yes, I Guess

Oh, the dish smashed
While the fish thrashed.
And wizards bewitched,
With a twitch and a swish,
Dishes to wish they could switch with the fish—

> Or so my father always tells me,
> Though I wonder: Should I trust
> A man who also fumes and fusses
> When I won't eat sandwich crust?
> (Not to mention how he's bothered
> By a speck of unswept dust.)
> But yes, I guess, I must believe him.
> Yes, I guess, I must.

Oh, the jars jump
While guitars strump.
At bizarre bazaars
Of busy old czars,
Tartars will barter for jars and guitars—

> Or so, at least, my mother tells me,
> Though I worry: Is it true?
> After all, she often uses
> Purple paint instead of blue

To help me watercolor oceans.
Sometimes green and yellow, too.
But yes, I guess, I do believe her.
Yes, I guess, I do.

Oh, the dog barks
While the frog craarcks,
And a frog in the bog
On a log in the fog
Joggles and boggles a boondoggled dog—

Or so I tell myself, but sometimes,
Late at night, I dream a hill
Is sweeping down the road, straight at me—
Then another and another, till
The rushing hills seem waves of water:
Green-dark oceans, never still,
All confused in tumbling motion,
Thrilling, chilling, spilling, shrill.

But yes, I guess, I will believe me.
Yes, I guess, I will.

2. My Fall

"School's neat,
Take your seat,"
That's what teacher said.
"Some fools
Like rules,"
I replied instead.
Hauled out.
Parents shout.
World gone sour and slow.
"Please, don't—"
"I won't—"
And back to school I go.

But the sky's not fooled, and the wind unschooled
Whispers through the trees
That the hills have seats where the air tastes sweet
And the long grass sways with the breeze.
For the leaves need lots of watching,
Tumbling as they fall.
And from the south the wild geese
Look back as if to call,
Come, come, come with us—
Dwindling with the fall,
Fading as they call.

"School's fine,
Stand in line,"
Teacher says next day.

I do,
It's true,
Listen and obey.
New pens,
New friends,
Timesing six by four—
New days,
New ways,
As teacher shuts the door.

But the unpenned wind in the open sky
Writes with whispered sound
Of forgotten joys and friendless toys
That played along the ground.
For the trees are always waiting
As light begins to fall.
And high above the yellow leaves
The wild geese still call,
Come, come, come with us—
Dwindling with the fall,
Fading as they call.

Feast of the Annunciation

We barricade this world against
The angels—try to keep at bay
Unwelcome news and admonitions,
Predictions of the coming day.

We block the way with laundry lines,
Curbside trees and privet hedge,
The crime-scene tape and bolted doors
That give our lives a stiffened edge.

Do angels cross the human border
The way that swimmers break the plane
From water's peace to mad disorder
And gasping air? The noise, the pain:

We are unfit for angels here.
Swift on his wings, Gabriel flies
To find—well, what? A willed confusion
Of hope and fear, and truth and lies.

Too much in motion, too much in mind:
The bus that bustles by, the cars,
The trains that run down tired tracks,
Back and forth, as blind as stars.

Our thoughts as well—stained with pride,
The clench of lust, ambition's schemes,

The ceaseless roar that still engulfs us:
Wrenching screeches, pulsing screams,

Till all the worn-down heart—the hurt
Abraded spirit—screams, *Be still.*
And once it was. *Let it be,*
She said, *according to Thy will.*

And with those words, all was changed,
All made ready, all prepared:
The pregnant pause, the sudden calm
That follows great decisions dared—

For remember: Mary *chose.*
This world, our souls, the baffled swirl
Of space and time—all holding poised
To hear that answer from the girl

Holding there, so young, so brave—
The blessed virgin who will draw
God enfolded in her flesh
And see the angels kneel in awe.

V: Spending the Winter

The Mermaid
Fenwick Island, Delaware

Fall comes too hard against this shore.
What little summer gave, we get no more.
A gray tide slaps against the beach,
And stilted houses brace for storms.
My daughter saw the dolphins reach
Once above the waves and disappear.
Along Cape May, the last boats steer
For winter berths and home.

The land is more inviting from the sea
Than sea will ever be from land.
What brought them out to dare the swell?
Long ago, men squared their sails
And sailed here from far away.
They sought the spume and ambergris.
They found the dying phosphate foam.
Europe spilled its seed upon the water,
And the water's sullen tide
Delivered us upon this shore.

America, my sea-born land,
The dark Atlantic's bright invention.
An osprey holds above the marsh,
Then drifts away along the coast.
We are alone upon the strand
And have no power left to boast
Of our escape from history—

Or history's escape to us:
This new world resurrected from the old,
This providential, chosen place
Preserved for God's experiment.
This almost Israel.

My daughter says a mermaid lives
Beyond the rocks that break the reef.
See her face, her hair, her clothes
In verdigris and greeny gold.
Among the sunlit waves she sings:

> *The wine-dark sea stains other shores*
> *Far from those a landsman knows,*
> *Where Father Triton blows his horn*
> *And breaks the backs of ships in storms.*

> *Come, sailors, I will bear you out*
> *To islands new with green delight,*
> *And I will show you worlds fresh born,*
> *Fair Bermudas made at dawn,*

> *And springs without a fall.*

A slow squall sleets across
The sun. Justice looks like this,
Once mercy's gone. Above the rocks
The seabirds scold as each wave breaks,
The thick swell slick with iridescent oil.
There is no recompense for toil,
Only punishment for idleness.
Hard consequence repays soft sin.

The noble meets the common death.
The good reverts to mean.
O America, my sea-born land.
My almost Israel.

We Meet Our Griefs

We meet our griefs again when work is through
    And do with words what little words can do.
A stranger weeps beside us through the night.
    Beneath our pleasant sun, we never knew
The dark that hates the day for being bright.
    We thought to build a garden without rue—
To climb and, all-beloved, to reach the height.
    Our faults were manifest: the false called true,
A petty discontent with wrong and right.
    For all such things we pay, but no sin drew
These hurts. It is our virtue they requite.
    Along the shore, the squabbling seagulls mew
At passing ships and wheel away in fright.
    We meet our griefs again when work is through.
We do with words what little words can do.

Homecoming

Sometimes I dream I'm flying
Just above the plain,
The world in wheat beneath me,
The rivers rich with rain.

And there I hear the murmur
Of what the old land knows:
All journeys need an ending.
All circles long to close.

My Grandfather's Table

The table in my grandfather's house
Was weighty and solid, sure of its place:
A walnut cave from which, little mouse,
To watch the serious, measured pace

Of all the big ones passing by,
The step of each grave, polished shoe.
And I would dream that I could fly—
Above their heads, beyond all view.

Slipping out past the windowsill,
I'd brush the leaves of the backyard tree,
Skimming the cemetery's hill
To reach clean air, unearthed and free.

Like great-winged hawks, grandfather and I
Would break away—and then we'd know
How to rise in the sunlit sky,
Not sink in shadows, down below.

The Mystery Writer to Her Detective

For you—policeman, brother, son—
I rule the way that all is done:
The gun misfires, your sister calls,
The bells in tall cathedral spires
Distract you when the gargoyle falls.
You'll find no accident transpires:
Your world reduced from mine until
It's frail enough I can compel
The time spent on a country drive,
The way the ways of the wicked thrive.
Beyond my study, children fall
And push each other on the lawn.
For you—policeman, brother, son—
I move a world that I've made small.

Sepulcher

Whose maul and chisel shaped this stone,
Who set the walls and lined with lead
These granite places for the dead,
I've never known. It's now my own:
A tended house of dry-laid stone

With quiet rooms for all my friends.
Those who drowned in distant water,
Those whose own hands made their slaughter—
All carried back to find their ends
In vaulted berths beside their friends.

And I have work here every day.
I sweep the walks and burn the leaves,
Tear dead ivy from old eaves.
I carve the name on each filled bay
And scour the rest, against their day.

Such tasks are nothing much to mind.
Their patterns leave no time to grieve,
And were I still, then every grave
Or happy memory would find
Unsealed loss to bring to mind,

And I would grieve again. These days,
With no new places for new friends,
I see at last where labor ends.
I'll latch the gate and find new ways
To wield my works, my hands, my days.

In Andalusía

In Andalusía, I saw the stars—
The stars, the stars, the Spanish stars.
Cathay's a dream Castilians dream,
America's a sailor's scheme.
Beyond these stars, things only seem.
In Andalusía, I saw the stars.

Spending the Winter

I know I need to get away,
Winterbound through each gray day
Or snowblind when the sun appears.
It rarely does. Time's in arrears.
Crankier each frozen morning,
The water heater groans in warning
That it will soon give up the ghost.
Nothing lasts in a winter post.

The banked coals stoked to grudging flame
Down in the blackened grate, I claim
A coffee cup to warm my hands
And watch the snow in the cold tree stands.
The dog soon whines to go outdoors.
The cackle of morning news implores
Cascades of fury: a murder spree,
A bribed inspector, a bargained plea,

A politician's knowing sneer,
The sycophantic crowds that cheer.
We have no innocence to save,
Only the sweaty boy who gave
Another boy the knife to end
The life of a third they'd called their friend.
Burn it all, scorch the earth,
And cauterize the human hurt.

But stop. Shake free. I turn away
From cabin-fevers of ashen day.
Our travel agent closed her shop
A year ago, but I still stop
Sometimes to stare at the posters there
And picture life in a warmer air—
A different breeze, a different dawn,
In places where the geese have gone.

It's just a fancy, the underclad
Beach scenes of a travel ad.
The tides will keep their undertow,
While here I stay to live with snow.
Through the window, I watch the sparrows
Scratch at suet. The season narrows
Down to sharp precisions—this
Cold spruce, this broken branch. This *this*.

The mind in winter may find a cleanness,
A keening wind to clear the meanness
Of skinflint soul and the chronic day,
A wind to tear vain thoughts away.
Self-concern, self-esteem,
Numbed and muted—till we seem
Nothing but a snow-capped field:
Draped in winter, smoothed and healed.

And rising to mind in this white age
I find the past, now free of rage,
Resentment, fear, all that had tinted
Memory before. New-minted

In winter's light, old scenes recur:
My grandfather's table, a stunted fir
On Delaware's rough shore, a throng
Of trellised roses, a children's song.

How they are is how they were—
Or near enough, as they refer
In pointillistic memory
To motes of the past as the past should be:
Nothing altered, nothing lost,
Nothing set beyond the cost
That we can pay. And I recall
The redolence of last year's fall,

My daughter running past spring blooms,
A summerhouse with sunlit rooms.
Near the Badlands, my father slowed
To point beyond the blacktop road
At red-tailed hawks on a gray-wood pole.
Though he is gone, that scene stays whole:
The ruffled hawks, the too-bright land,
A dusty windshield, his pointing hand.

The dog is barking to come back in,
And I must move with the now, again.
Each daily need, each daylight chore,
Keeps us in time, like a music score.
But still sometimes a cold eye sees
A sparrow break for the snow-dressed trees.
Together the bird and its memory climb—
The recompense of wintertime.

Notes and Acknowledgments

Most of these poems are previously unpublished, but some earlier versions have appeared: "Easter Morning" in *Grace Notes*. "The Hidden Life" in *The Formalist*. "The Morning Watch" in the *New York Sun*. "Saro's Love Song" in *Post Road*. "Reading by Osmosis" and "Tardy" in *First Things*. "The Mermaid" in *Crisis*, dedicated to Michael Novak. "We Meet Our Griefs" in the *Weekly Standard*. A recording of "Homecoming," set to music by Michael Linton (as part of "Dakota Wind"), was released by Refiners Fire Music, and "Some Come to See the Lord" by Remodeled Music. "Feast of the Annunciation," commissioned for an Oratory dedication in Ave Maria, Florida, later appeared in *Vineyards*. "Four Seasons," commissioned by Phi Beta Kappa of Princeton University for their 2022 ceremonies, was printed as a limited-run chapbook by David Sellers at Pied Oxen Printers.

A note on the text: "Floret Silva Nobilis" reflects its start as a translation of the macaronic verse (Latin with bits of Middle High German) of the same name in *Carmina Burana*, before it drifted into its current play between Romance and Germanic sources of English. "The Morning Watch" owes its narrative flow to Manuel Bandeira's 1927 Brazilian poem "Profundamente," and "O Portuguese" borrows some thoughts from Olavo Bilac's 1919 sonnet "Língua Portuguesa." "Saro's Love Song" builds from an online Kurdish satire by Sardasht Osman (under the penname *Saro*), given a literal translation into English by Aryan Baban and Michael Rubin; the Kurdish original helped lead to Saro's murder. "The Logician's Lament" uses the valid syllogistic form *Darapti* (AAI-3): *All hair is red, All hair is warm, therefore Something warm is red.* "An Adulterer's Introspection" references "the curious incident of the dog" in Arthur Conan Doyle's 1892 Sherlock Holmes story, "The Adventure of Silver Blaze." The cover illustration is E.J. Austen's "The North Wind and Elfie," *St. Nicholas* magazine (1891).

Far too many friends were importuned for help along the way, but Justin Blessinger, A.M. Juster, Len Krisak, and Sally Thomas contributed more than even friendship can hope. The composer Michael Linton was always ready to talk about musical settings. Conversation with Ari Bernstein has been a joy. The classicist Joaquín Dominguez Arduengo has been a sane and helpful interlocutor about ancient poetry. My friend David Goldman is the pattern of those who have stood by me through the years. The poet Rhina Espaillat remains an inspiration.

The founder of St. Augustine's Press, Bruce Fingerhut, always believed in my work, joined now by publisher Benjamin Fingerhut and editor Catherine Godfrey. The support of José-Marie Griffiths, president of Dakota State University, has been a comfort, as has the support of retired provost Richard Hanson and former dean Benjamin Jones (now South Dakota's official state historian)—the trio who arranged for me an academic perch. The current dean, the sinologist David Kenley, has continued the school's kindness.

The generation now slipped away stays in mind, and much of my work reflects the intellectual and personal debts I owe them: René Girard, Richard John Neuhaus, Gertrude Himmelfarb, Hugh Ormsby-Lennon, Michael Novak, Ralph McInerny, Avery Dulles, and many others. *Orate pro eis, ut pro nobis orent.*

As ever, my wife Lorena and daughter Faith were constant in love and support. Even our dog Hades contributed, insisting by his presence on a canine poem. But as is only right, this book is dedicated to Heather Hyde, who took me in when I was very young and became my mother.